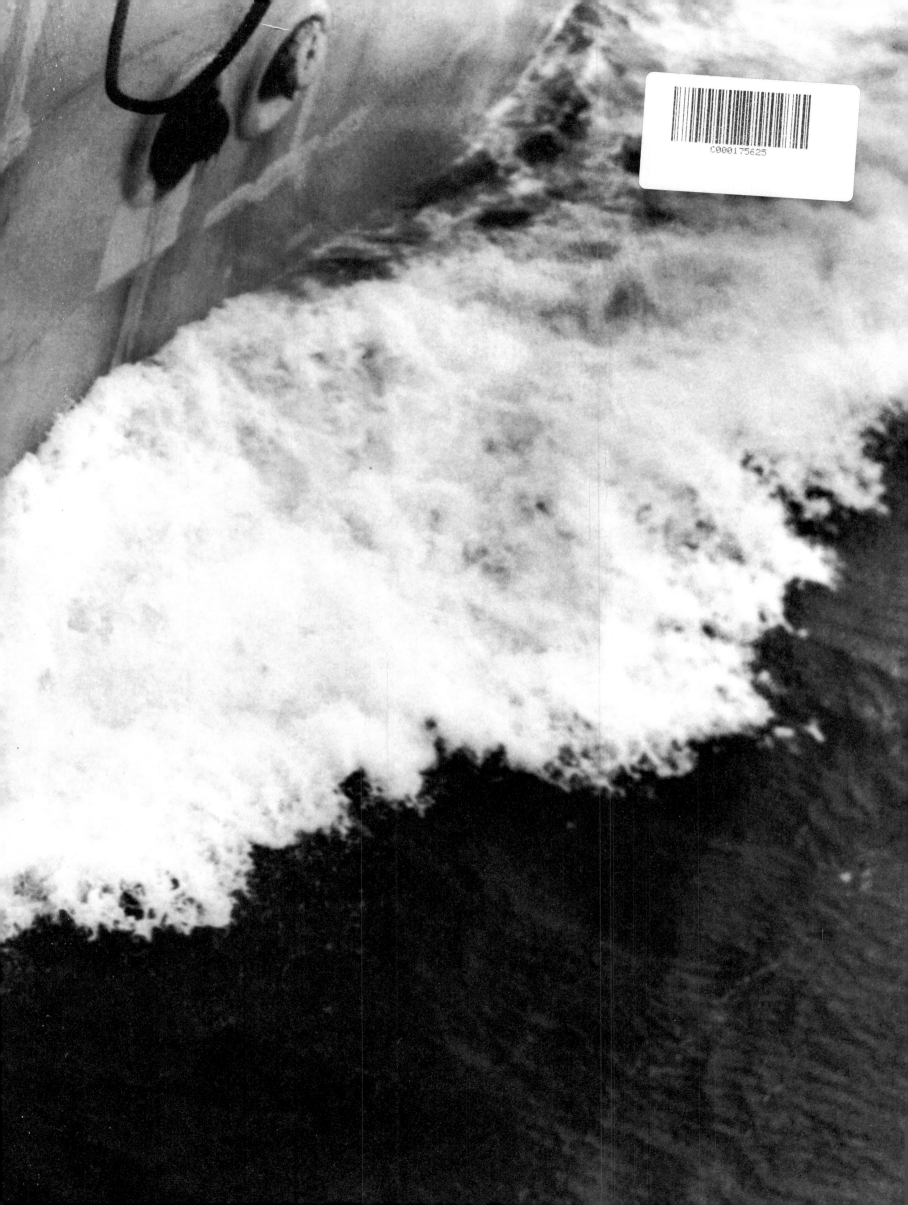

THE LAST OF THE WIND SHIPS

INTRODUCTORY TEXT BY BASIL GREENHILL

PHOTOGRAPHS BY ALAN VILLIERS

EXTRACTS FROM PUBLISHED WORKS BY ALAN VILLIERS

THE HARVILL PRESS, LONDON

First published in Great Britain in 2000 by

The Harvill Press
2 Aztec Row, Berners Road
London N1 0PW

www.harvill.com

FIRST EDITION

The following texts by Alan Villiers are quoted in this work:
Falmouth for Orders, first published by Henry Holt and Company, 1929
By Way of Cape Horn, first published by Geoffrey Bles, 1930
Voyage of the Parma, first published by Geoffrey Bles, 1933
Last of the Wind Ships, first published by George Routledge and Sons, 1934
The Set of the Sails, first published by Charles Scribner & Sons, 1949
This edition © Nancie Villiers, 2000
Introductory text © Basil Greenhill, 2000
Photographs © The National Maritime Museum, Greenwich,
The Alan Villiers Collection

The authors have asserted their moral right to be identified as the authors of this work

A CIP catalogue record for this title is available from the British Library

ISBN 1 86046 799 7

Designed and typeset in Janson and Copperplate by Crook and Cash
All photographs hand-printed by Melvin Cambettie-Davies at Master Mono, London
Map and line drawings by Reginald Piggott, Norfolk
Originated in Italy by Sele Offset, Turin
Printed and bound in Italy by Artegrafica, Verona

CONTENTS

INTRODUCTION BY BASIL GREENHILL

I. THE HERZOGIN CECILIE VOYAGE
With extracts from "Falmouth for Orders" and "The Set of the Sails"

II. THE GRACE HARWAR VOYAGE
With extracts from "By Way of Cape Horn" and "The Set of the Sails"

III. THE PARMA VOYAGES
With extracts from "Voyage of the Parma" and "Last of the Wind Ships"

PHOTOGRAPHIC CREDITS

ALAN JOHN VILLIERS 1903–1982

M any, many years ago, as a 15-year-old boy in the 1940s, I spent a summer afternoon or two lying propped on my left elbow on the granite margin of a slipway down to the high water mark at Marazion in West Cornwall in England. I was reading a book I had borrowed from a commercial lending library at Penzance, visible across the bay. The book utterly absorbed me. It was titled *By Way of Cape Horn* and was an account, written in 1930, of a particularly nasty passage from South Australia to Queenstown, the harbour of Cork in the Irish Republic in the Finnish steel full-rigged ship *Grace Harwar*. Its author was an Australian seaman turned journalist by the name of A.J. Villiers.

The book was written by a man with the background and experience of a seaman in the big steel square-rigged sailing vessels which had become virtually obsolete as merchant ships in the Western world before the First World War, long before the passage of the *Grace Harwar*. A.J. Villiers described a kind of life and technology best expressed as "the sailing culture", a culture which had been an important influence in Western thought for centuries. The book's power and authority came from the author's professionalism, both as a writer and as an old-style seaman, but also from his remarkable energy and passionate involvement with these great vessels. Even a boy could feel that.

A.J. Villiers explained something of why the *Grace Harwar*, a maritime dinosaur, was still generating capital for her owners, sailing, if you like, on the margins of the international maritime economy, 30 years after the last of such ships had been built in Britain. This, it appeared, was a result of the then "Third World" economy of the Åland Islands, a Swedish-speaking archipelago community, part of Finland in the Baltic Sea. Its port town was Mariehamn, where the *Grace Harwar* was registered as a merchant ship.

A week or so after my afternoons on the slipway, my mother and I sailed over to Penzance harbour. Here there was a small, handsomely shaped wooden motorship discharging timber. On her stern was carved her name and home port, Torborg, Mariehamn. There was a sudden sense of reality. A passage to the Baltic two years later in the *Viking* – a steel four-masted barque and a sister ship of the *Grace Harwar* – followed over the years by long journeys in many different merchant ships, was to confirm my lifelong involvement with the study of maritime history.

ALAN VILLIERS ABOARD THE *GRACE HARWAR*

Alan Villiers was born in 1903 near the wharves in Melbourne harbour where the ships discharged their cargoes. By the time he was three the family had moved to another house, a two-storied building with a balcony from which the docks could be seen. Australia in those days was dependent on shipping for its development and there were plenty of merchant sailing vessels to watch. Wooden schooners and barquentines from the West Coast of North America could still make a good living in the specialised trade of carrying lumber across the Pacific to build the wooden houses of growing Australian cities. Big barques and full-rigged ships, although in rapidly reducing numbers, still brought timber from the Baltic ports of Finland and Sweden and loaded wheat and wool for ports in Britain and mainland Europe.

Various uncles took young Alan for walks in the docks to see the ships from close quarters. It was the big barques which became the centre of his attention, the large iron and steel square-rigged vessels of the last stage of sail in merchant shipping which lasted from the 1870s to the 1890s. His most impressionable teenage years were during the First World War when, with a world shortage of tonnage, old sailing ships began to earn single freights equal to the whole value of the ship in 1914. This was the last time these deep-sea merchant sailing vessels of Britain, Scandinavia, France, Canada and the United States were profitable investments, the last boom in sailing tonnage when a ship could double in value while making a passage at a good rate. It didn't last, of course. By 1921 the bottom began to fall out of the market. Owners who had made fortunes with old vessels in 1917 and 1918 quickly disposed of them if they could find buyers in 1920. Later investors were almost always ruined.

But by then Alan Villiers had committed himself to a life at sea and not merely to being at sea, but to mastering the sailing culture, although that very culture was dying in front of his eyes. His father, a tram driver in Melbourne, was a man of great energy and talent, highly intelligent and humane in outlook, who became deeply and actively involved in the labour movement. The family were poor but Australian society in the early 1920s lacked the inhibitions and class barriers of Britain at that time (and much later) and saw it as quite natural that the clever son of a tram driver should get a scholarship to Melbourne University and enter the profession of his choice. This was Alan's father's ambition for him. But the sailing culture, as a practical reality, had him in its grip.

When his father died of cancer, Alan was only 15, but he was already steeped in his father's standards of integrity and social responsibility. Hard as it may have been at times to maintain them, these became part of the man as did an ability always to view his fellow human beings in a favourable light. His father's death meant poverty for the family and the end of Alan's ambition for further education. Leaving school, he worked in a local factory and sought a way of going to sea to learn the handling of a sailing vessel. In the end he found a route through an organisation set up by retired master mariners, all products of the sailing culture, to prepare boys for sea through weekend courses and then find berths for them in the few old sailing vessels which still managed to pay their way in the trade across the Tasman Sea between Australia and New Zealand. Alan joined one of these, an old barque named the *Rothesay Bay*, which carried boys as apprentices, and began his training to be a professional seaman, as he thought and planned, in sailing vessels.

The steamship, which ultimately brought an end to the great age of the "wind ships", took roughly 70 years, from 1815 to the 1880s, to develop fully and her progress depended on industrial developments which took place not at sea, but in engineering works and shipyards ashore. Until the fuel-efficient "compound" engines were created in the 1870s, steamships were simply not offered for more than a very limited number of ocean trades. There was no "battle" between sail and steam, and sailing vessels carried the bulk of the world's trade.

Even after the developments in steam power of the 1870s the shipping world remained uncertain of the way forward. World trade for over two decades continued to be shared between the new efficient compound-engined steamers and the sailing ships which, under the stimulus of real competition for the first time, were very rapidly improved in design and economy of operation. Using the engineering techniques developed for steamships, larger and larger sailing vessels took advantage of the economies of scale, and were built, first of iron and then of steel. A few examples of these big vessels survive although they have been much adapted for training purposes, at "tall ships" rallies today. It was not until the 1880s that steam tonnage registered at British ports finally and permanently exceeded sail tonnage. The great steel four-masted barques, whose striking and handsome appearance when seen under sail so caught the imagination of the young Villiers, remained an economic proposition for a generation or so. But after the late 1890s they ceased to be built. At long last the steamship came of age.

The economics of sail no longer made sense. The last big sailing vessels built in the 1890s cost very roughly £22,000 old currency or so to build – approximately £9 or £10 per ton, £500 at early twenty-first-century prices. By 1907 they were selling for £4 per ton, by 1910 for £2. At the end of the wartime boom when Villiers was seeking a berth they found very few buyers at all. Alan Villiers, therefore, grew up in the years of the tail end of the sailing vessel and its culture; an extremely complex culture, as he soon learned in the Tasman Sea trade. It took years of experience, gained in isolation from the life on land and spent in total absorption in the many aspects of the craft, to become a master of it. At the beginning of the 1920s no ambitious young man in search of a sea career stayed in sailing vessels. Villiers in the Tasman Sea joined old ships run on the breadline and manned by elderly men with no future. But, of course, as an idealistic teenager filled with ambition to become master of a great square-rigged ship he did not see this. Remarkably, he was to achieve his ambition.

Brought up in poverty in early twentieth-century Melbourne, Villiers did not find any particular hardship in the squalor and endless grinding hard work of life in the *Rothesay Bay*. In fact he gloried in it and rapidly acquired the skills to be rated ordinary seaman in his next ship, the barque *James Craig*. She had been hulked – stripped of her spars and topmasts and moored as a floating coal store in a New Guinea harbour – before the First World War. In the wartime boom she had been re-fitted and re-rigged and employed in the hard trade across the stormy Tasman Sea between Australia and New Zealand. Alan thrived on the life in what was a very well run vessel. She inspired, in his autobiography, *The Set of the Sails*, a statement of a deeply held belief:

> *"It seems to me that the foc's'le of a happy sailing ship at sea was one of the most pleasant abodes of a labouring man where the sailors of all nations had learned through the centuries to work and live amicably together. Here was true democracy."*

But in the post-war depression she was sold out of service to be hulked again. That episode was not to be the end of her story. At the beginning of this century she lies, re-rigged and re-fitted once more, as a museum ship in Sydney harbour.

When he signed off the *James Craig*, came the time for Alan to sign on a big four-masted barque bound for Europe, preferably round the legendary Cape Horn. He did so aboard a British vessel, the *Bellands*. She was not a happy ship. Years later Alan wrote about her,

> *"A good ship handled sloppily is an aggravation to men who take a pride in their calling and are ready and profoundly happy to take a pride in their ship also… The voyage was, at any rate, a good object lesson in what not to do if I ever became a sailing-ship captain myself, as I surely proposed to do… the unfortunate Bellands suffered from a malady… poor officers."*

In London he began the search for another ship. The war was over and deep depression had set in. World trade was sluggish and there was a surplus of available tonnage. Continental ports were full of sailing vessels awaiting a buyer. Alan was now on the first rung of the professional ladder, desperate to continue his ambition to conquer the sea. There was no future whatsoever in big merchant sailing vessels in the developed world, as we would now call it, and he would never be the master of a fine four-masted barque. The only future at sea was in powered vessels which were no part of his ambition. But he was on the verge of an experience that was to lay the foundations of a very successful life which, extraordinarily, was always associated with sailing vessels. To understand what happened it is necessary to explore in a little detail something of the history of the 6,000 Åland Islands lying in the Baltic Sea midway between Stockholm and the coast of south Finland.

Finland, which now has one of the most sophisticated economies within Europe, was still in the 1920s a relatively poor country, largely reliant on forestry and marginal agriculture. The Åland Islands, lacking capital, were dependent on small farms and sailing ships in world trade. Åland lies almost on the 60th parallel of latitude. The sub-Arctic climate is harsh and unforgiving. Conditions in Åland can be rigorous and the result is an exceptionally hardy and resourceful population – for generations a people of the sea who now own and operate a large merchant fleet which includes some of the world's most sophisticated vessels of their type. The 25,000 or so people are a privileged minority within a minority, a self-contained, self-perpetuating group whose Swedish language and culture are secured by the successive Autonomy Acts of the Finnish Parliament.

Long circumscribed in their maritime activities by total lack of capital and by Russian trading restrictions – Finland became a Grand Duchy of Russia in 1809 – the Ålanders for generations sailed small, locally built wooden vessels, called in Swedish *galeaser*, to Stockholm and to the Finnish mainland and traded in firewood and farm produce. With the profits of the contracts for the building of a great Russian fort at Bomarsund in the heart of the Islands, capital accumulation began and following the Crimean War of 1852–56 the Russians began gradually to relax restrictions on maritime trade. In due course bigger Åland-built vessels penetrated first the North Sea then the Atlantic and soon the world. The Russians allowed the building of the port town of Mariehamn in 1861 with full trading rights and in time a fleet of medium-sized wooden square-rigged vessels was built up. By the time British owners began to dispose of larger iron and steel sailing vessels at low prices at the end of the century Åland owners were in a position to buy them. They had the business experience and international connections necessary for the successful operation of the ships. One of the most important of these connections was with H. Clarkson & Co., shipbrokers in London specialising in Scandinavian shipping matters.

In the early twentieth century some Åland shipowners built up fleets of sailing vessels which could be operated profitably because lack of alternative employment ensured readily available skilled local crews inured to hardship by life in the sub-Arctic. There were strong seafaring traditions, much respect for master mariners and a social cohesion of the community that meant that there was relatively little crew trouble. The ships were bought cheaply and overhead expenses remained very low as the ships were managed from rooms in the private houses of the owners.

"It is strange, this mixture of farmer and Cape Horn master-mariner which Åland has produced. All the holder masters in these Cape Horn ships are interested in farms on their native islands, which remain the one place on earth where the old maritime traditions of places such as Main, old Tasmania, and the older English ports still hold. Åland is entirely farming and marine, and its maritime interests are almost wholly concerned with sail. Boys there may still begin their sea careers in fishing barques, and from these move on to deep water and Cape Horn, their officers' certificates and ultimate command. There they still attain command long before they are thirty and are second mates at nineteen. They have their own navigation school, their own ships, their own traditions, and their own sea style. The islands, which appear to be one or two on small-scale maps, really consist of a group of some six thousand rocks, islands, islets, and sea-surrounded pieces of territory, scattered in such profusion that the ordinary farm, away from the principal island, usually consists of anything from 6 to 300 islands. Thus it was necessary for the farmer, if he wished to till his soil, to be something of a mariner too, since he had to travel by water from field to field. Here he grew things in such profusion that he had to find an export market for them ... he soon made a success of that business and of little ships: so he progressed from the Gulf of Bothnia to the Baltic and the North Sea, and so to deep-water ships and the world."
(Voyage of the Parma)

When vessel prices went through the roof in 1916–17, the major shipowners of Mariehamn disposed of the ships and moved to other forms of investment in mainland Finland. This left many smaller owners and two on a relatively large scale, the Lundqvists of Wårdö, and a new man, baptised Gustaf Adolf Mauritz Gustafsson. As his shipowning grew he was to simplify his name to Erikson. His family were prosperous farmer-shipowners and he sailed in their ships as boy, as bo'sun and mate, and in 1899 gained his deep-sea master's certificate of competence. He bought shares in vessels and became principal owner and master of a newly acquired Canadian-built barque named *Southern Belle*. After further experience in command of larger ships and by then a shareholder in nine vessels, at the age of 41 he retired to the family farm. But farming was not to be his future.

GUSTAF ERIKSON, LAST POWERFUL OWNER OF THE GRAIN-TRADING WIND SHIPS

At the outbreak of war in 1914, Åland's 26 large iron and steel sailing vessels were all outside the Baltic. There were appalling difficulties of management and communication – the vessels were legally Russian and Russia was at war with a Germany which controlled the Baltic. Freight rates – pre-paid before the vessel sailed so they could at once be invested in further tonnage – multiplied by five times and were paid in currencies not affected by the wartime inflation of the Russian rouble. Gustaf Erikson had set up a small shareholding group around his home village to buy an old Dutch barque, the *Tjerimai*, intended to be run in the North Sea timber trade. In August 1914, she was outside the Baltic and so was able to profit in deep-sea trade from freights which, by 1917 when Finland broke away from Russia and became an independent country, had multiplied eleven times on 1914 rates. His very large personal gains were ploughed back into more sail tonnage and by 1919 he had acquired seven big iron and steel vessels.

Erikson, who had found he had a great business flair, together with the Lundqvists and some smaller shipowners bought sailing tonnage at post-war depression rates. One of these vessels was the *Lawhill*, an old British steel four-masted barque. In 1921 she discharged a cargo of Australian grain in Bordeaux. Through Clarkson's, Alan Villiers was signed on for a passage from Bordeaux to Port Adelaide for orders at 430 Finnmarks per month, while the Åland able-seamen were signed on at 900 Finnmarks. In due course for four months' and one day's work he drew 1815 Finnmarks (then less than £18) but he had four months' more sea time in sail and a superior rating on his record. He was, at the age of 17, a real professional and able to hold his own with the Ålanders both as a seaman and, rapidly, in the Swedish language principally used on board.

He was the only man on board not of Finnish nationality and almost the only non-Ålander. At that time it was very unusual for an Åland vessel to sign on such a man for an outward passage from Europe. The *Lawhill*'s small crew, although not experienced in big ships on deep water, was made up of lads from farmer-sailor families who were well educated, enthusiastic about their profession for which Finnish law still demanded extensive preparatory experience in sailing vessels and very keen to speak English. Villiers grew to value all his shipmates, some of whom became companions from one ship to another.

> "I found the Aaland islanders pleasant young fellows, with whom it was easy to get on. Few spoke any English, but Lusitania continue to be an excellent friend and mentor... I was welcome because I was another hand, and because they could learn some English from me. More than that, I like the innate sense of real democracy, the insistence on genuine fair dealing, which I always found to be part of the Scandinavian character, at any rate among sea-faring man."
> (The Set of the Sails)

This was a long way from the international flotsam who too often made up British sailing-vessel crews at that time. Although the very happy account he gives of the *Lawhill* in his autobiography may reflect Alan Villiers' later involvement with the Åland community, it is evident that he got on well in the socially cohesive and democratic organisation of the vessel and gained very valuable experience and contacts which were to serve him well later. Alan Villiers did not know it but he joined the *Lawhill* at an auspicious time. The *Lawhill*'s success saved Erikson's business and enabled him to continue as a shipowner.

Meanwhile Alan Villiers was at a crossroads in his life. It would appear from the company records that his association with the *Lawhill* had been intended simply as that of a seaman working his passage home. He was no doubt a very useful man on board and was offered another passage as able-seaman on full pay but the *Lawhill* experience was a turning point. While the social microcosm on board the *Lawhill* had greatly impressed him, the Alan Villiers who returned to Australia was not the boy who had left the country. He now understood that there was no possible future for him as master of a large square-rigged sailing vessel and that his undimmed enthusiasm for the sailing culture must have other ends. But what was he to do? An accident on board a few hours after the *Lawhill* made her Australian landfall, hitting a sand-bank, had left him temporarily handicapped.

> *"And immediately, too, the forefoot of the big ship came up on the beach, as she hit Australia with a gentle thump which quivered the masts and all the rigging. Caught off balance, working with two hands, I was pitched from the yard and hurtled to the deck. I was so surprised that I had no time to be frightened. One moment I was working away, full of pleasurable thoughts. Next moment, the rigging was flung past me, and a tar-covered wire hit me a grazing clout. I felt myself strike other rigging. Then the deck. It seemed to me, in a last instant of consciousness, that the deck was surprisingly soft. It was not the deck that was soft. It was I."* (The Set of the Sails)

Unable to find work as a seaman, he "decided to leave the sea and go to Hobart in Tasmania and begin life afresh". Life afresh consisted of a number of temporary labouring jobs followed by the extraordinary conviction, at the initiative of a friend, that he could become a journalist.

> *"A newspaper reporter? Why, this was just the thing for me! Until then I had never thought of journalism as a profession I could enter. The Labour journals for which my father wrote paid nothing, and dealt only in propaganda. I had not realized that young men were employed to report news... It came to me almost with the suddenness of a bombburst that newspaper reporting was just the thing that I could do."* (The Set of the Sails)

Alan took typing and shorthand courses in the evenings and eventually obtained a very junior job on the *Hobart Mercury*, an influential provincial newspaper. However, he saw little prospect of breaking out of it into a reporter's job for which years of seniority were needed. He was now a very mature 19 and driven by latent energy and ambition. It was 1922.

Traditional whaling until the First World War had been carried on largely in relatively temperate waters. This was the whaling of the great American classic, *Moby Dick*. The Ross Sea, a great indentation in the coast of Antarctica, had been the base area for a number of Antarctic expeditions of what is now called the heroic age of exploration. Amundsen had used it to gain access to the continent for his brilliantly conducted journey to the South Pole, Scott for his less well-conducted journey to the Pole and heroic disaster. These and other pre-First-World-War expeditions had reported great numbers of whales in Antarctic waters. Seeing the opportunity, a Norwegian group took a sizeable financial risk and fitted out a different kind of whaling enterprise. Having obtained permission and a guaranteed five years' monopoly, they acquired a fleet comprising a mother ship, an old steamer renamed the *Sir James Clark Ross*, and five little whale chasers and sent them south to see what could be made of the Ross Sea whales. This whaling venture had stirred great interest in Australia and New Zealand. Alan Villiers saw his opportunity and grasped it. The whalers were in Hobart for only a few days during which he convinced the *Hobart Mercury* to let him act as their correspondent for the expedition.

THE *SIR JAMES CLARK ROSS* AND THE FIVE LITTLE CHASERS WHALING IN THE FROZEN SOUTH

"On November 30th, 1923, I sailed from Hobart in the whale factory-ship Sir James Clark Ross ... *This was the first modern whaling expedition into the Ross Sea, which previously had been visited only by scientists and explorers ... Sometimes whole miles of the Barrier crumbled away without warning, and tumbled into the sea, a lovely cascade of shining blue-green ice which shimmered and scintillated as it fell, but set up the devil of a sea and made the flensers leap for their lives. Sometimes blizzards got up suddenly and hurled frozen snow horizontally in our faces, and the decks were a shambles of blubber, grease, and frozen blood. Steam from the blubber boilers covered everything with ice. The whole ship looked frequently as if she had been carved out of the ice, too, and would remain down there for ever, solidified into a dreadful berg."* (The Set of the Sails)

He was equipped with a fine camera and signed on the Norwegian mother ship as whalers' labourer at £4 a month. His shipboard Swedish from the *Lawhill* was near enough shipboard Norwegian for him to get along – he was very quick to pick up a working language. The life and work was gruelling, filthy and cold, but, characteristically, he loved it. The stories he sent from the sea as "Australian Press Correspondent with the Expedition" through the ship's wireless telephone were sold around the world. This was good for the Norwegians and very good for the *Hobart Mercury*. He returned from the ice to be promoted to junior reporter without further apprenticeship. He had found what was to be his road in life – seafaring, writing and photographing.

Alan settled down to working as a reporter. His old-fashioned sailor's ability to get on with all manner of people, a real flair for presenting a story in a vivid, human manner, coupled with energy and initiative in pursuing a story resulted in rapid promotion and within no time, he was a senior reporter. He expanded his Antarctic articles into a 100,000-word narrative and produced *Whaling in the Frozen South* which was immediately published in England with considerable success and subsequently in America.

I bought my own copy of the American edition of Alan Villiers' first book at a used bookstore down on the East Side in New York City in 1954. Alan later wrote in it, "To Basil, with apologies! I don't think I've written quite such a bad book since!" In fact it was a remarkable first work for a 22-year-old seaman turned reporter. He evoked the experiences of writing it in his autobiography, *The Set of the Sails*.

> *"When my reporting was finished that day, I went straight home and sat down in front of the typewriter. Within a day or two I had finished the book, as if the printer's devil had been at my elbow screaming for the copy. I had acquired the habit of working quickly – too quickly – from the newspaper training. I had no idea then of the ghastly permanence of the published book, no nightmares – as I should have – of the hastily written thing following through the years, haunting me, sneering at me. So you rushed me through the typewriter in a couple of days, did you? Clever fellow! And how do you like reading me now? Can't stand it!? No wonder. If you only learned not to do the like again, perhaps it wouldn't be so bad. But did you? DID YOU?"*
> (The Set of the Sails)

The book dealt with life and work so exotic and so totally new to most readers that even today it has strong interest and remains a valuable piece of Antarctic history. Whilst Alan remained ashore, his brother Frank had taken to seafaring, sailing in Åland ships, and he was keeping Alan in touch with developments in their unique shipowning ventures. For Alan the building blocks had all slipped into place for his third career, which in its early stages produced the magnificent photographs in this book.

When Alan joined the *Lawhill* as a 17-year-old able-seaman at Bordeaux in 1921 the master of the vessel, who had played a role in saving the Erikson business, was a man named Ruben de Cloux. He came of an old Åland family and was a much respected figure as well as an employee who did not have to dance to his employer's tune. When the *Lawhill* arrived in Bordeaux he was anxious to return to his farm, north of Mariehamn, which he had seen little of for many years, but in July 1921, Gustaf Erikson wrote to him offering a salary nearly double that of any other master in the fleet. If despite this, Gustaf wrote, he must quit the sea for a while, then he was asked to stay on board until his chief mate, J.E. Gustafsson, had formally taken over command on promotion. It was during this interregnum that young Villiers came on board with his introduction from Clarkson's and the astute de Cloux must have noted such an unusual new crew member. As things turned out de Cloux was to be one of the most important figures in Alan Villiers' early adult life. After sailing with him in the *Parma*, Alan Villiers wrote,

> *"He was without doubt a great deep-sea sailing ship master, at his best when his whole energies were required for his ship and he was the driving force which made her passages... I had had the*

opportunity to learn under a great master who had shown, time and time again, that he could get more out of square canvas than any other man then in the trade. He was a magnificent seaman and it was a privilege to be his partner and to serve with him." (Voyage of the Parma)

In 1921, a number of war prizes still lay in French hands in various ports including Ostend. Amongst them was a former Norddeutscher Lloyd cargo-carrying training ship, the *Herzogin Cecilie.* This beautiful ship could be a very good investment for Gustaf Erikson. In the end, after long and complex negotiations he was able to buy her at a give-away price. She was, to use a translation of an Åland phrase, to "sail in" a fortune for him over the years. For most of the first nine of these, Ruben de Cloux was her master.

In 1927, 24-year-old Alan was sent by the *Hobart Mercury* to Melbourne, then the capital, to attend an Australian inter-state conference. In dock there was the very visible *Herzogin* discharging Baltic timber. Alan went on board and, visiting the big saloon in the after part of the long poop, met again the master, Ruben de Cloux.

The four-masted barque *Beatrice*, a Swedish cargo-carrying training ship, had challenged de Cloux to a race to Europe once the two vessels had loaded their cargoes of Australian grain. A Swedish paint company had promised a trophy for the winner. "It was obvious that the coming 15,000-mile race . . . ought to be as good a story as I had stumbled upon when I shipped in the *Sir James Clark Ross . . .* I arranged to ship with him for the coming passage toward Europe, as able-seaman, at six pounds (Australian) a month." This was the only occasion on which the annual lift of grain from South Australia to Europe by Åland vessels was associated with a formal race. It led, however, to the creation by the media of an annual "Grain Race" which focused the public's attention in the 1930s. These were never "races" in any formal sense although the crews of vessels naturally took pride in a good passage.

Alan knew that there was a job to be done investigating the market for Tasmanian apples in Britain and northern Europe. "I put it to the editor then, that for six months' leave, my job back, and one hundred pounds towards expenses, I would get myself to England and the

MANNING THE YARDS ARMS ABOARD THE *HERZOGIN CECILE* (LEFT); THE
AUSTRALIAN STOWAWAY JENNIE DAY WATCHING THE *C.B. PEDERSEN* APPROACH

Continent and make a detailed survey of fruit marketing conditions for his newspaper. He jumped at the idea, as well he might." Alan's voyage was secured.

The *Herzogin Cecilie* was built as a crack cadet ship for a great German steamship line. She was built and fitted out to the highest standards. Not only was she a cadet ship and cargo carrier, she was a floating ambassador and show ship for the Germany of the Second Empire. Because she was a cadet ship she had no labour-saving devices to help with the handling of the running rigging. The heavy hauling work, inevitable in a sailing vessel, was good drill and exercise for the trainees. In 1913 German records show that in addition to the master and mates she carried seven experienced petty officers, 39 able-seamen, 22 ordinary seamen and 22 cadets, a total of 90 men. She was designed to be worked with almost unlimited manpower. Her crews after 1922 were less than one-quarter of her design complement. On the passage she was about to start she had a total crew of 26.

Villiers bought a folding camera and was to write many years later, "... [my] venture in photography aboard the whaling ship had turned out well, and it was obvious that there was an excellent and almost untouched field in the Cape Horn sailing ship. I have never spent thirty shillings more wisely in my life."

The passage of 96 days to Falmouth was a good one. De Cloux drove the great barque very hard when the weather allowed. When it did not, "de Cloux clung to every stick of sail, and the yards were trimmed to every slightest variation in the breeze. Nothing but perfection in his sail-aerofoils was good enough for de Cloux. With nine hands in a watch, perfection was a hard taskmaster." Alan was now 24, as fit and tough as ever, and he took to the life again immediately. A few days out, however, they discovered with horror that there was a female stowaway. And when the vessel discharged her cargo in Cardiff she became the object of intense media attention. There was greater interest in her than in the ship or the race with the *Beatrice* which the *Herzogin* won hands down. Unwittingly, Miss Jennie Day made a considerable contribution to the growing fame of the *Herzogin* and to world awareness of Åland ships. Alan Villiers devoted one-tenth of the book he wrote during the passage to the stowaway incident and the story no doubt contributed to the book's considerable success. Published in 1929 as *Falmouth for Orders*, it went into several editions over the years and had a great effect in stimulating public curiosity about these last great "wind ships". It records a way of life and work which would now be not merely impossible, but also illegal in the West. But through it all comes Alan Villiers' deep professional commitment to the sailing culture which was his mainspring in life. His passion for his subject is clear, as is his deep happiness with the life on board – a life that was completely strange but fascinating for the great majority of his readers.

Falmouth for Orders made the *Herzogin* something of an international phenomenon. The last British-owned big square-rigged steel-built sailing vessel, the *William Mitchell*, had been broken up in 1926 and really large sailing vessels, spectacular and handsome as they were, were becoming rarities. The Western world was becoming aware of them and the *Herzogin*, one of the most spectacular survivors, attracted attnetion in the press, on the radio and on cinema news reels whenever she sailed. Like many other aristocratic refugees she succeeded in retaining her dignity despite the transition from crack cadet ship to merchant vessel.

Alan Villiers' reports on the apple trade were very well received in Australia and during his travels he diverted to the Åland Islands. He saw nothing of the glorious archipelago countryside where the farmer-shipowners had created the shipping industry, but only Mariehamn.

Gustaf Erikson gave him a brief interview in which he typically presented himself as a saviour of sail, rather than as a very able shipowner exploiting a peculiar local situation. Alan told me years later that he thought him as hard a case as any he had known in his youth, nor did he respond kindly to Alan's questions about undermanning. He might well have done. As a result, largely, of Alan's book, articles and lectures, youths from all over the world were ready to pay large fees for the experience of shipping in an Erikson vessel. Not only was any manpower problem solved but the profitability of the ship was increased. Nevertheless, Alan liked Erikson.

"He was a small man with a limp and a somewhat aggressive way of speaking. His countenance was rugged and square… His eyes were keen blue… He had two great and opposing ambitions – one that his ships should be kept up magnificently, and the other that no money should be spent on them… A moment or two's conversation was sufficient to make me realize that his affection for big sailing ships was a very real thing, though he might be making a handsome profit out of them.
(The Set of the Sails)

Alan returned to Tasmania after three months in Europe to find himself with possible careers as a politician or in journalism on the mainland. He chose neither. He had another idea. His magnificent photographs of these last great ships should be supplemented before it was too late by a documentary film. Alan and a fellow reporter, Ronald Walker, had been toying with the thought for some time. When they heard of the arrival of the *Grace Harwar*, the last Cape Horn full-rigger in the Australian trade, Alan decided "it was time to leave Tasmania".

THE *GRACE HARWAR* LOADED WITH GRAIN BOUND FOR FALMOUTH AND CARDIFF BY WAY OF CAPE HORN IN 1929

"We wanted to make a picture that would capture some of the stirring beauty of these ships, that would perpetuate, in the realm of shadows at least, something of the glory of their wanderings and the courage of their battles with the sea; that would embody, in some vague and unsatisfactory way, some shadow of the spirit of these lovely old sea wanderers, some glimmer of understanding of the attraction which they hold over those who sail in them. It had never been done."
(By Way of Cape Horn)

They raised the money to buy two cameras and 6,000 feet of commercial film, which was all they could find on the Australian market. They deliberately shipped in the *Grace Harwar*, 40 years old she was being run down before being sold to breakers. Little money had been spent

ALAN VILLIERS AND APPRENTICE ELISABETH JACOBSEN, PRESUMABLY ON BOARD THE STEAMSHIP THAT TOOK THEM FROM NEW YORK TO SIDNEY EN ROUTE TO THE *PARMA* IN JANUARY 1933, CALLING AT HAVANA, THE PANAMA CANAL, HONOLULU, SAMOA, FIJI AND AUCKLAND.

on her for some time. She had the usual very small crew. Alan and Ronald Walker chose her because she represented the old type of big merchant sailing ship without mechanical aids for handling the sails and rigging, with a long open main deck (unlike the *Herzogin*) and with no protection for the helmsman at the open wheel. The film would show old-style seafaring. It did. They had experienced a passage from hell. Walker was killed in the rigging. The second mate went mad as a result and jumped overboard in bad weather but was miraculously rescued. She was grossly under-provisioned and they were always hungry. She was, of course, under-manned. They never had enough sleep, were never warm until the tropics, were rarely dry and the work was appallingly hard. Scurvy developed.

> *"We were forced to lead a monkish sort of life, undernourished, fighting adversity with insufficient rest. A full belly is no aid to reflection. Our near-empty bellies, week after week, sharpened our minds. We were forced to find our souls, if we had no knowledge of them before. We were forced to accept in humility the help of God, or we could not have gone on. There was no escape, and there were no distractions. Yet I know I was never clearer-headed in my life. I was one of a handful of able seamen in a heavy ship, grievously undermanned. I steered. I pumped. I worked aloft. I often sewed sails all day on deck, and worked with them in the rigging half the night. I did what I could to help the second mate. I filmed and photographed, for that could not be given up, and I tried to make as good a job as Walker would have done. When the weather was good, I brought out my battered portable typewriter, and got on with my maritime history of Tasmania, for that had to be ready for press when we came in."* (The Set of the Sails)

Finally they signalled a tanker in the North Atlantic which sent a boat with meat and vegetables. At that time they were becoming too weak to work the ship but characteristically Alan shot all 6,000 feet of film. Alan wrote of Karl Gottfred Svensson, master of the *Grace Harwar*:

> *"He acted like a good officer with a group of men in a front line trench, whom he well knew to be up against it. He was a quiet pleasant spoken man, and he looked like anything rather than a popular conception of a Cape Horn master mariner... I understood before very long, just why that strange young captain regarded his boy-crew as front line soldiers, for such they were, in a ship which tried them almost beyond endurance."* (By Way of Cape Horn)

After the *Grace Harwar*, pained by the death of Walker, Villiers was out of love with ships and the sea and quickly got a good job with an Australian news agency in London. He wrote *By Way of Cape Horn*, the book I read as a schoolboy. Looking at it again now I can see why it gripped my adolescent imagination. It marks Alan's maturity as an author. A powerful, straightforward narrative of a prolonged and dreadful experience, it quickly became a bestseller, described by the press as "... one of the most remarkable records of sea travel in the English language".

With the journey came another success: on board the liner which spoke with the *Grace Harwar* in the Western Approaches had been Dr Gilbert Grosvenor, President of the National Geographic Society of America. The publicity about the book and the film came to his attention and Alan was asked to do an American lecture tour. He had a direct down-to-earth lecturing style which went perfectly with his subject and the tour, and others which followed over the years, was a great success. Alan found himself in possession of some small capital and a link with the prosperous *National Geographic* which was to stand him in good stead until the end of his life.

In June 1929 Ruben de Cloux resigned his command of the *Herzogin*. The reason he gave Gustaf Erikson – that he wished to be at home for a while – was not the full truth. His daughter, Ruby, told me years later that he had tried to persuade Gustaf Erikson to sell him shares in vessels, but Papa Gusta kept the shares exclusively for his own family. And so de Cloux had watched Erikson and the Lundqvists amass fortunes under Åland conditions from the operation of obsolete sailing tonnage. He had for a long time been considering acquiring a sailing vessel with a shareholding group of relatives and neighbours in what had been the normal way in Åland before the First World War. He would be master. Germany had for many years been a great consumer of nitrates mined in Chile and used as fertiliser and in chemical manufacture. This was a business which, like the South Australian wheat trade, involved the slow and erratic loading of cargo and German sailing vessels were operated in it until artificial nitrates ended it in the late 1920s. Then the barques were disposed of. Erikson duly bought a couple.

In 1930 there was another, the *Parma*, lying in Hamburg for sale. She could carry 5,300 tons of cargo and could with luck be run profitably for several years until she needed major maintenance, whereupon she could be disposed of at a scrap price as good as her purchase price. A group of ten family members and neighbours and Gustaf Erikson, whom it was politic to let into the enterprise but not as a majority shareholder, was formed. Fifty-one percent of the shares were held by the de Cloux family, but in fact 19 percent of these shares were held by Alan Villiers. The *Parma* was purchased in October 1931 for about £2,000 – roughly £100,000 today.

Extraordinary as it may seem, the totally obsolete *Parma* sailing under Åland conditions in the 1930s proved to be a sea-going gold mine. The day after she was bought she was fixed for a cargo of 5,000 tons of Australian grain at almost four times the investment in the vessel. Next season's freight earned her £370,000 at 2000 prices. Having made some capital, Villiers then sold his shares back to the de Cloux family two years later. As part-owner he spent his time learning everything he could from the vastly experienced de Cloux. Alan had learned to have enormous respect for de Cloux whom he described as the "best sailor in the world".

Alan wrote a book, published in 1933, about the first homeward passage of the *Parma* under Åland ownership. They had a bad time in the Southern Ocean and Alan's description of an exceptional storm was mesmerising and could have been written only by a professional seaman and a brilliant journalist.

"From mast to mast, yard to yard, clewline to downhaul, buntline to leachline, the wet-through boys toil, taking in sail after sail. Some come in easily, but the mains' is deep and a devil to roll up on the yard. All hands on a yardarm cannot make much impression on it until there comes a lull; the wind tears at them and the hail beats them, while their sodden oilskins, useless against wind, sea, and rain, flap about their ears and the heavy canvas billows out before them with an area that seems as vast as the sea itself. Now finger-nails go and curses fly, and young lungs roar with the effort of the fight. Many of the boys seem badly off for gear, as real sailors have always been. Some have no oilskins, others no seaboats, and none of their hard-weather suits looks fit to stand up to a Cape Horn rounding. Several of them have such rags of clothing that, even in this bitter weather, the bare skin shows through. I doubt if any came from the rigging dry."
(Voyage of the Parma)

THE *JOSEPH CONRAD*, ACQUIRED BY ALAN VILLIERS IN 1934 AS A TRAINING SHIP

"I decided to make a voyage round the world, an ambling circumnavitation by way of Good Hope and the Horn, the East Indies and the South Seas; and to ship all the young fellows who cared to come and there was room for." (The Set of the Sails)

But there are differences from the earlier books. This is a book written from the poop rather than from the forecastle, a book from a successful man of ever widening experience and sophistication and a growing international reputation and it shows. The photographs have gained in maturity; he has sharpened his gaze and mastered the subject. Before *Voyage of the Parma*, as the new book was called, Alan had published under the title of *The Sea in Ships* a book of 112 of the photographs he had taken on his passages in the *Herzogin* and the *Grace Harwar*. Such was its success that it was followed by *Last of the Wind Ships*, a book of over 200 photographs of the *Parma*'s passages, which rapidly went into three printings.

The photographs were beginning, in the early 1930s, to attract wide attention perhaps more for their pictorial beauty and exotic interest than for their great value as a unique record of a maritime way of life of an earlier period of industrial and social development. They are, of course, all these things and today we recognise the many dimensions of their value. Alan photographed throughout this period almost entirely with the very simple folding camera, a Kodak 120, that he had bought for the *Herzogin* passage, often working under extreme conditions. By the standards of today it was utterly primitive. Alan always disavowed any knowledge of photography, saying that all he did was to point the camera and press the shutter release, always choosing a good light, yet he produced work of outstanding beauty.

Alan's interest in the *Parma* had paid off and he once again found himself with capital. In the belief that experience in a well-run sailing vessel, preferably square-rigged, was likely to be enjoyable and very beneficial for boys even though they had no intention of following a sea career, Alan embarked on a new venture. Who else had ever in modern times taken a full-rigged ship around the world as a private venture? In 1934, Alan bought the Danish training ship *Georg Stage*, a very beautiful little full-rigged ship of just over 200 tons which was to be replaced

SAILING ABOARD THE ARAB DHOWS IN THE LATE 1930S (TOP)

"A Kuwaiti deep-sea sailing boom looks its best under full sails. This is Ali Nejdi's famous boom Bayan *on its annual voyage bound for the East African coast."*

YOUNG BOYS TAKING A BREAK ABOARD AN ARAB DHOW (LEFT)

"Mariners aloft bending the sail. The lateen yard is brought in more or less vertically so that they can get at the sail. They shin up like monkeys: there is very little to hang on to." (Sons of Sinbad) (RIGHT)

in Denmark by a new sailing vessel. He re-named her *Joseph Conrad*, after the novelist whom he greatly admired, and in three years sailed her by very devious routes around the world with an international crew of cadets, officered by Ålanders. The lovely *Joseph Conrad* was, in fact, more typical of the sailing ships of history than were the great steel barques. He published a book, *The Cruise of the Conrad*, and a second book of photographs of the circumnavigation, *The Making of a Sailor*. Once his journey came to an end, he sold her to a millionaire in New York in 1937 for twice what he had paid for her in 1934. She is now to be seen at Mystic Seaport, Connecticut.

> *"Not a boy or a young man trod the* Conrad's *decks who did not benefit by that voyage; and now I had to sell her to a rich young man who proposed to convert her into a yacht for his personal use, the kind of ship I most detested, the good ship turned harlot to be an idle piece of well-proportioned scenery at selected anchorages in the right season of the year. I had sailed round the world to deliver a 'yacht' to a Fifth Avenue millionaire, who would provide no opportunities for the training of youth, and would immediately set about putting power in the vessel, and chromium-plated bathrooms. I hurried away to sail with the Arabs in their deep-sea dhows across the Indian Ocean, for there are no chromium bathrooms in an Arab dhow."* (The Set of the Sails)

Forever fascinated by the ocean's great wind ships, Alan embarked, in 1938, on what was to be a programme of five years' investigation of the sailing culture as it was still practised in the Near and Far East. The scheme was cut short by the Second World War but he lived for a year or so on board Arab vessels and wrote the best account of them and the life around them that has ever been published. He called the book *Sons of Sinbad* and it is a remarkable account of the life in a sailing trade which had lasted for centuries. Sailing wooden dhows in the Indian Ocean was a long way from the *Herzogin Cecilie* but Alan took to it with his usual enthusiasm and determination and learned and recorded more about this exotic business than any European before him.

In the Second World War Alan became a temporary commander in the Royal Navy in charge of squadrons of landing craft and was awarded the Distinguished Service Cross. After the war he sailed, at the invitation of the Portuguese authorities, with their fleet of white-painted schooners in the North Atlantic cod fishery. He received a Portuguese decoration and had a fine new fishing vessel, the *Alan Villiers*, named after him. Once more this experience produced an outstanding book and a film.

He commanded the replica of the "Pilgrims" ship *Mayflower*, built at Brixham in Devon, and sailed her across the Atlantic to the berth where she still lies at Plymouth Plantation in Massachusetts. He made the passage into a kind of archaeological experiment and we learned much of the problems of shiphandling faced by seventeenth-century mariners. He advised on ships and shiphandling for the production of major feature films, *Moby Dick, Billy Budd, Hawaii*. He broadcast and televised on both sides of the Atlantic, and became a media personality so well known that when I walked with him through the streets of Edinburgh in 1959 people would stop us and ask to shake his hand. He had no illusions about this ephemeral interest and he had a nice disrespect for the world of entertainment which had captured him and which limited opportunity for the exercise of his considerable talent as a scholar of history.

I had first met Alan at a gathering of an academic society in London in 1946 and we found that we shared many of the same ideas. One was the urgent necessity of establishing a national

ADVANCED NAVIGATION CLASS, "SHOOTING IN THE SUN", ABOARD THE *JOSEPH CONRAD*

collection of historic photographs of merchant shipping. We found others of like mind and, with Alan as chairman, we constituted ourselves as a committee of unofficial friends of the National Maritime Museum with the object of encouraging the collection of photographic records. Half a century later the result is probably the greatest archive of its kind in the world. It would be proper for the present generation of Trustees of the Museum to name it "The Alan Villiers" Photographic Library.

This would be all the more appropriate as most of his photographs are deposited in the museum as are some of his films, which are dubbed with his own spoken commentaries. Alan was a trustee of the museum for many years. In the 1960s I escaped from diplomacy into the much more congenial job of the museum's director. Alan was a powerful ally and support in the fascinating work of reconstructing a rather moribund institution as the world's major museum of its kind.

Alan settled with his Australian wife, Nancie, whom he had married in 1940, and their three children in what he called "Dons' Alley", in a big house in north Oxford. Nancie frequently accompanied him abroad and helped his work enormously until the end of his life. They never returned to Australia to live. The University of Melbourne, where he once intended to study medicine, awarded him the honorary degree of Doctor of Letters. That institution also holds his library of 5,000 volumes. He continued writing until his final illness forced him to stop.

Alan's last book was a short, simple explanation of the handling of square-rigged ships. Called *Voyaging with the Wind*, it suggests that Alan in his years of Oxford prosperity was faced with a personal dilemma. His writing, lecturing and broadcasting and particularly his three-year sail-training voyage with the *Joseph Conrad*, led to a worldwide interest, not only in the last Åland ships but in sail training and in sailing in large vessels as cruise ships. Through his writings the big square-rigged sailing vessel had become, as she remains today, part of Western mythology. But when Alan thought of sail training his conception was of the total submersion in the sailing culture necessarily involved in handling merchant sailing ships. Modern sail training, with some notable exceptions, conducted in vessels with powerful engines as well as their rigs, sailing to tight schedules and providing relatively brief, highly structured experience against a modern Western social and economic background is quite remote from the old life in merchant vessels. Although he had perhaps been able to synthesise it to some extent in the *Joseph Conrad*, the world of which Alan in his boyhood had experienced the very tail end no longer existed when he wrote his last book. His ideals could now no longer be fulfilled.

Modern sail training, although very relevant to twenty-first-century conditions, is not nineteenth-century seafaring. Today men and women have assumptions, ideas, values and standards of material comfort quite remote from those of men whose way of life, indeed of survival, was encompassed by the sailing culture. They cannot ever share Alan's experiences in the *James Craig* or the *Lawhill* because they do not see the world as he and his fellow professional seamen saw it then. Alan not only left us an unparalleled and most valuable visual record of the very last years of the old life at sea, in his person he bridged the old world and the new.

Alan Villiers, as a fine seaman, epitomised the precept of an earlier master, that "you must know the sea and know that you know it, and not forget that it was meant to be sailed upon". Other men have been fine seamen and written good books, although seldom in so happy a combination; but what made Alan unique in his generation was an idea and an achievement quite different from anything that his contemporaries had in mind. He was a tough realist. "No man," he wrote, "takes to the sea life naturally. The good seaman would be as good or better in other fields" – as he was himself. He was, to use his own words of *Joseph Conrad*, "a noble and high-minded man with great ideals and determination". He saw something to be done which seemed to him good and, being born at the right time, he did it.

The few surviving big steel square-rigged merchant sailing vessels of the types in which Alan Villiers made his photographs in the 1920s and 1930s have been re-masted, re-rigged, sometimes just for cosmetic effect, converted into training or cruise vessels, floating restaurants or museum ships. Some of the museum ships have been very well done. Alan Villiers' boyhood home, the *James Craig*, lies properly restored in Sydney and the visitor may appreciate something of what life must have been on board her as a working vessel in the Tasman Sea nearly a century ago. The *Joseph Conrad* at Mystic Seaport has been completely re-fitted below decks but her masts, spars and rigging are properly maintained as they were on her round-the-world voyage under Alan's command. There remains only one big sailing vessel which survives unchanged and well maintained as she was as a working merchant ship. She is the four-masted barque *Pommern*, a sister ship in the Erikson fleet to the *Herzogin Cecilie* and the *Grace Harwar* and she lies, splendidly maintained – even to a complete set of sails with all their gear – on the waterfront of Mariehamn's Western Harbour alongside what is perhaps the world's best museum of regional merchant shipping. She is just as she came in from the sea in 1939 at the end of her last passage from Australia – by way of Cape Horn.

Basil Greenhill,
Boetheric, January 2000

THE VOYAGES 1928–1933

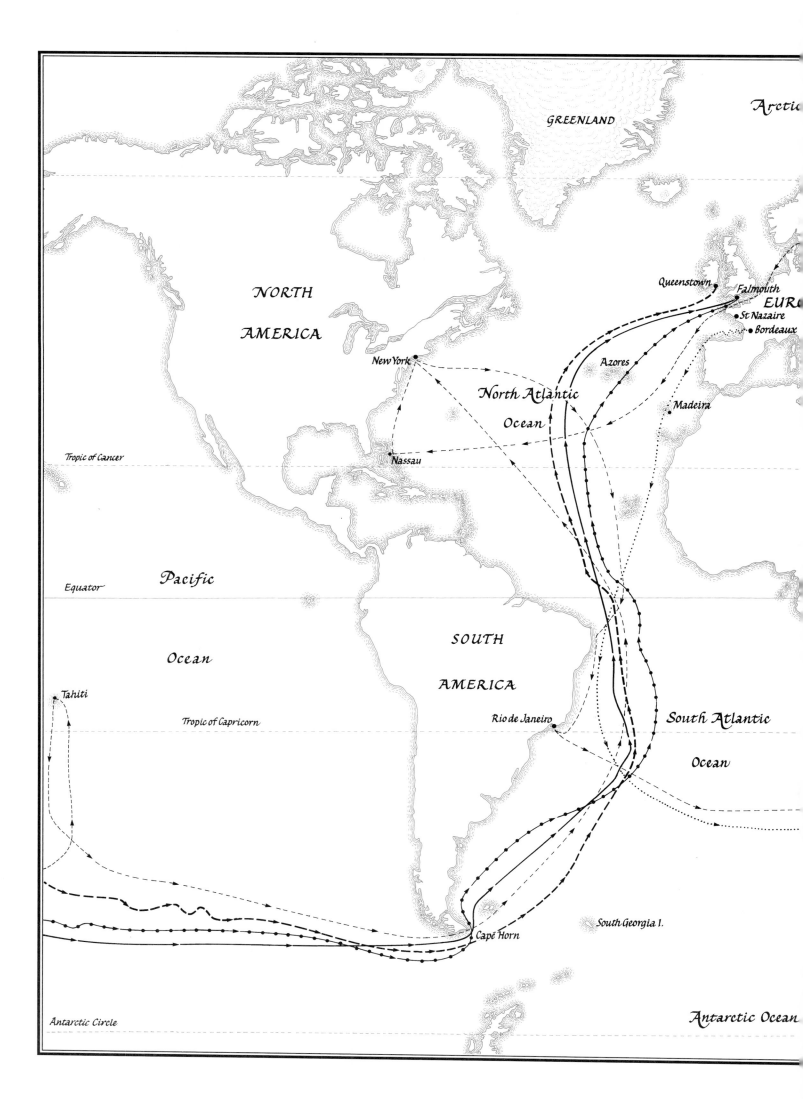

GREENLAND

Arctic

NORTH

AMERICA

Queenstown

Falmouth

EUR

St Nazaire

Bordeaux

New York

Azores

North Atlantic

Ocean

Madeira

Tropic of Cancer

Nassau

Pacific

Equator

Ocean

SOUTH

AMERICA

Tahiti

Tropic of Capricorn

Rio de Janeiro

South Atlantic

Ocean

South Georgia I.

Cape Horn

Antarctic Circle

Antarctic Ocean

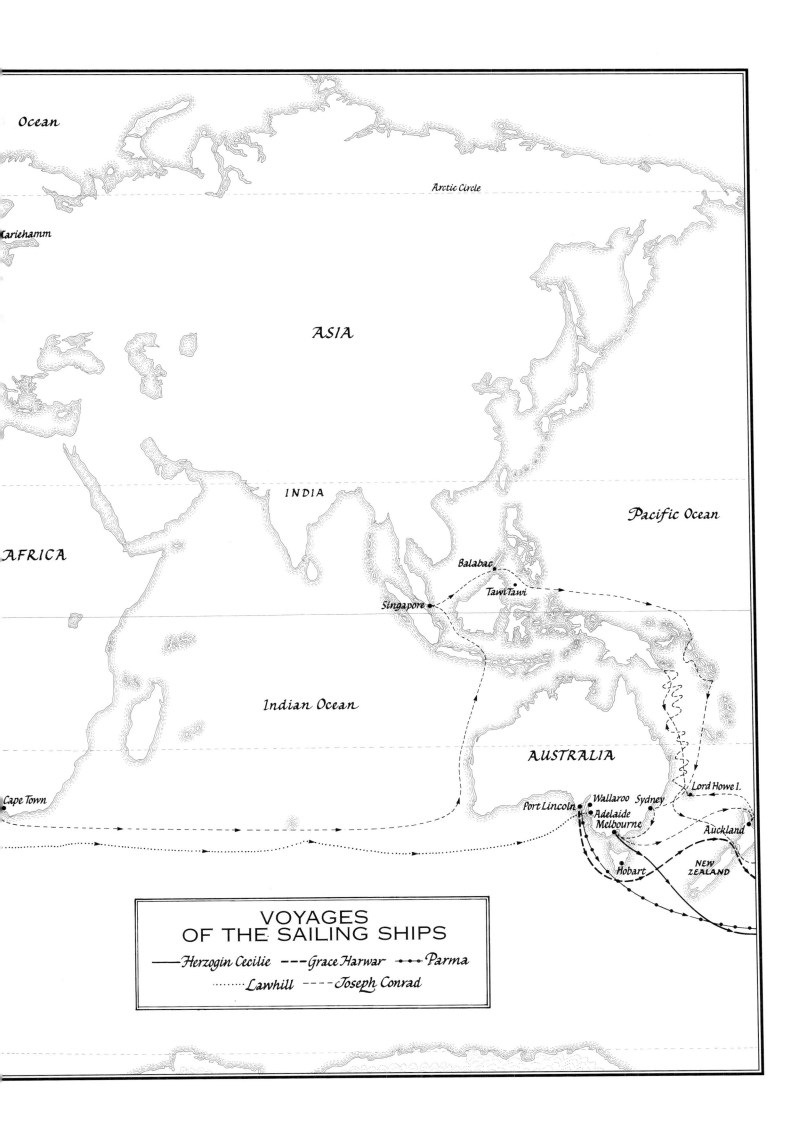

Ocean

Arctic Circle

Mariehamm

ASIA

INDIA

Pacific Ocean

AFRICA

Balabac

Tawi Tawi

Singapore

Indian Ocean

AUSTRALIA

Cape Town

Lord Howe I.

Port Lincoln Wallaroo Sydney

Adelaide
Melbourne

Auckland

Hobart NEW
ZEALAND

VOYAGES
OF THE SAILING SHIPS

—— Herzogin Cecilie - - - Grace Harwar •-•-• Parma

·········· Lawhill - - - - Joseph Conrad

FOUR-MASTED BARQUE
SAIL AND RIGGING SHOWN WITH ALL
SAIL UNBENT ON THE MIZZEN

A. Bowsprit
B. Foremast
C. Mainmast
D. Mizzen mast
E. Jigger mast

1. Flying jib
2. Outer jib
3. Inner jib
4. Fore topmast staysail
5. Foresail
6. Fore lower topsail
7. Fore upper topsail
8. Fore lower topgallant sail
9. Fore upper topgallant sail
10. Fore royal
11. Main royal
12. Main upper topgallant sail
13. Main lower topgallant sail
14. Main upper topsail
15. Main lower topsail
16. Mainsail (shown hauled up in its gear)
17. Main topmast staysail
18. Gaff topsail
19. Spanker
20. Mizzen royal yard
21. Mizzen upper topgallant yard

22. Mizzen lower topgallant yard
23. Mizzen upper topsail yard
24. Mizzen lower topsail yard
25. Crojack yard (or Crossjack)
26. Main stay
27. Mizzen stay
28. Jigger stay
29. Braces (Called by the yard to which bent:
    thus, 'Royal braces', 'Topgallant braces,' etc.)
30. Main brace
31. Capstan
32. Anchor
33. Fore sheet
34. Galley
35. Charthouse
36. Spanker boom
37. Wheelhouse
38. Counter
39. Cutwater
40. Figurehead
41. Bobstay
42. Bowsprit end (showing lucky shark's
    tail nailed there)
43. Gaff
44. Main truck
45. Forecastle

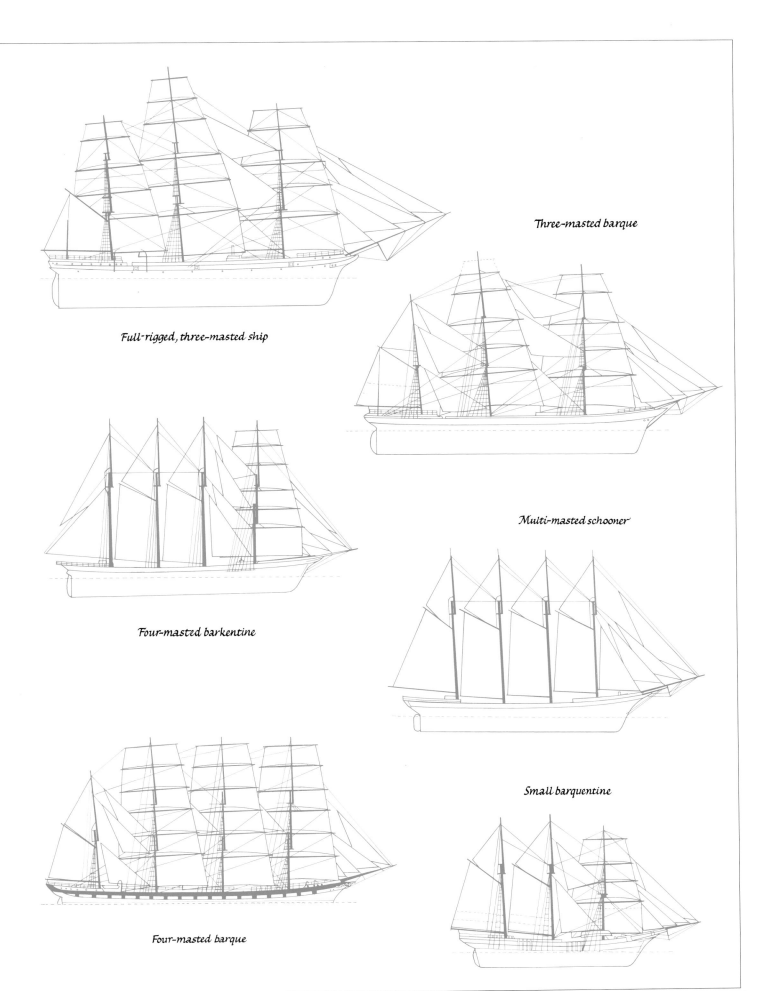

Three-masted barque

Full-rigged, three-masted ship

Multi-masted schooner

Four-masted barkentine

Small barquentine

Four-masted barque

HERZOGIN CECILIE

"HERZOGIN CECILIE" WAS BUILT AT GEESTEMUNDER IN 1902
AS A TRAINING SHIP FOR THE GREAT NORDDEUTSCHER LLOYD CO. OF BREMEN
STEAMSHIP LINE, AND IN THAT COMPANY'S SERVICE SHE REMAINED
UNTIL THE WAR PERIOD. SHE PASSED TO THE FINNS, IN 1921, AS PART OF
THE ERIKSON FLEET. SHE WAS A POWERFUL, LOFTY, STEEL FOUR-MASTED
BARQUE, OF 3,242 TONS, REGISTERED IN MARIEHAMN WITH CAPTAIN DE CLOUX
AS HER MASTER. SHE LOADED GRAIN IN 1928 AND RACED AGAINST
THE "BEATRICE" FROM PORT LINCOLN TO FALMOUTH FOR ORDERS,
WINNING IN 96 DAYS.

2   BECALMED, VIEW FROM THE SHIP BOAT
(PRECEDING PAGES)

"We made one memorable use of that long spell of light winds and
calm. We put out a boat, one day, and took photographs of the ship.
She lay stagnant upon a sea of dull and glassy calm, heaving slightly in
a long swell that was not caused by wind. There was no wind in the
sails; there was no progress in the ship, no motion – except her gentle
roll and gentle dipping – no life. And yet she was the most gloriously
beautiful thing that any of us had ever seen at sea. [...] We loved
our ship the more after that – though we had loved her well before –
and we did not growl about the calm. For we knew that we could not
complain if the sea held her to gloat upon her glory. It might not have
the chance for so very long."

3   GOING ALOFT THE FORE MAST

"To climb from the fore-deck to the fore-royal yard takes a smart
sailor three minutes; it would take a landsman thirty – if he could get
there. From such an eminence one gets a real idea of the beauty of
the ship's lines and the height of her masts. Her main-yard is over a
hundred feet long, and if her foresail were spread in the Strand there
would be a traffic jam that would take all day to clear."

18   THE SLEEPLESS OCEAN

"We had always our sunsets and our sunrises, and all the beauty of the sea spread lavishly for us alone to see. [...] The sailing ship sees many strange things at sea, things that have a simple enough explanation if only one knew it, I suppose – queer streaks of light in the water, extraordinary contortions, curious misshapen masses going by in the distance, marvellously shaped fish that show an evil head above the water for an instant or two, then to disappear for ever, leaving one wondering if they ever were really there."

19   AT THE MIDSHIP'S HELM IN FINE WEATHER (OPPOSITE)

"She is more than a ship to the sailor in her focs'l; she is a personality. He knows her; he has watched her make her voyage, has seen her come bravely through a hurricane, haul safely off a lee shore, work miraculously through a calm. He has studied her little ways, the eccentricities and the peculiarities which each sailing ship has to herself; he knows what she can do and what she can't; he knows when she is being asked to do too much and when too little. He always speaks of his ship as if she lived."

"Sail-making went on constantly, for the open space beneath the poop provided a magnificent sail loft. De Cloux was the best sailmaker in the ship, probably in all the surviving sailing ships, and it was customary for all the able seamen and everybody else who could wield a needle to lend a hand with seaming. All the sails were handsewn, every inch of them. Cutting a new sail was a work of art, and only de Cloux and the sailmaker himself put a knife to new canvas. It was de Cloux's aim to sew a complete new suit of sails every two years, and that meant handling more than 40,000 square feet of canvas and miles of heavy wire and tarred hemp rope."

The Set of the Sails

"The idea of the wind-using vessel remained – and still remains – fudamentally sound. Perhaps, if the last lesson to be administered a softening civilization be not too final, there may be a realization of that fact yet, and the commercial sailing ship will be revived. It is devoutly to be hoped that this may happen before the last man with practical knowledge of the sailing of such ships has passed away.
Man created the deep-sea square-rigged ship, and she was in many ways his loveliest creation – certainly his most beautiful, upon the sea. She was a loyal, a faithful, a competent, and a valuable servant.
At her best, she was a poem in canvas, a glorious symphony of the sea. At her worst, she was frequently better than her designers intended, and always more than a full affair of steel, and cordage, and sails.
In her, modern man discovered all that was discoverable from the sea, and opened up the trade routes of the world. She bred a race of seamen who were incomparable – courageous, reliant, invincible sailors, whose souls were in harmony with the elements they understood and used. They were in truth men who went down to the sea in ships. They knew ships and they knew the sea. Now they have gone; and a later kind of man has banished the ships they loved from the oceans of the world. What man created he has also destroyed. The loss is his, and it may yet be a serious one."

6 VIEW FROM THE BOWSPRIT, WORKING ON THE PORT
ANCHOR (OPPOSITE)

"There was little of good weather or of kind skies to be expected from
the Cape Horn road at any time, and winter was now rapidly coming
on; it was as well to forget such things as sunshine and happy warmth
from the beginning, and not to think of them until the South Atlantic
came, months later, and we crossed the Tropic of Capricorn and came
into the Trade-winds. [...] Not for her any soft pursuit of good
weather and mild routes, for the benefit of pampered passengers. For
her there is no consideration save winds; she is not concerned with
the distances she may sail, but with the winds she meets. She does not
seek good weather, but bad; she does not look for peaceful days, but
stormy ones, for these help her on. She calls at no ports, and makes
no deviations. She has no aim, save to reach her destination. She has
no work, save the safe delivery of her cargo. With this end nothing
can matter, even if it be the lives of some of her crew."

FOLLOWING PAGES IN SEQUENCE

7 SHE LISTS AND HEELS TO THE WIND BUT STILL RUNS
ON AT SPEED

"In the evening the ship rose and fell gracefully to the caress of the
seas, bowing to their majesty ere she set out on her months-long fight
with them, while they lapped around her grey old sides, and kissed
her in a kind of cold welcome; and as the wind freshened and the
night came, fumed and hissed and roared around the sweet cutwater,
and swept along angrily astern, where the deep bottom had cleft
them. They broke grudgingly before the figurehead and leapt with
wild exultation over the focs'l head, and across the fore-deck; when
the ship rolled, with her steady old gracefulness, they skimmed closely
along her t'gall'nt rail and spilled a little of themselves aboard, on
occasion, not as if they really meant to, yet, but just to let us know
what we might expect from them afterwards. The main deck was wet
upon the first night, nor was it dry for months afterwards."

8 HAULING ON THE BRACE AT THE MAIN MAST

"The first week out is a bitter experience, with nothing much of
romance about it. Somehow the voyage seems a ghastly business,
then, and the sea ahead appears interminable. You realize the full
significance of the task before you – to be blown by the wind from
Australia to England! To be subject to every puff of wind, every squall
that blows, through four months or more, over fifteen thousand miles
of ocean! To have to work by the strength of your hand a full-rigged
ship, dependent upon her sails alone for her motion, round Cape
Horn to England! It is something, when you get first out to sea, and
think about it; it means something, when the land had slipped into the
obscurity of the haze astern and will not emerge again from the haze
ahead for four months or so – and perhaps never. [...] The constant
hauling on wet ropes and straining with wet, wind-stiffened canvas is
very hard on the hands and makes them cruelly sore, whether one has
come from office desk or pick and shovel. All our hands were quickly
in the same condition, freshest greenhand and oldest shell-back.
Deep, bloodless cuts and splits in the flesh appeared in the palms and
along some of our fingers, and remained there malignantly, even if
one tried to do something about them. They never healed, and never
made any change, except sometimes to be more painful. Our wrists,
from the constant frapping of the frayed oilskin stuff bound closely
around them, became red-raw and exquisitely painful; our oilskins
quickly became sodden and useless."

"We wanted to make a picture that would capture some of the stirring
beauty of these ships, that would perpetuate, in the realm of shadows
at least, something of the glory of their wanderings and the courage of
their battles with the sea; that would embody, in some vague and
unsatisfactory way, some shadow of the spirit of these lovely old sea
wanderers, some glimmer of understanding of the attraction which
they hold over those who sail in them. It had never been done.
[…] There would be, in this film of ours, 'shots' of the rolling,
sea-swept decks of the sailing ship down below New Zealand on her
way to Cape Horn; the great seas would sweep aboard her over
each side as she rolled, sweeping triumphantly along the length of her,
pressing her down, weighing heavily against her in the fight to stay
afloat; and in all this there would go on the endless battle with the
sails, the braces, the heavy, back-breaking gear – the puny things with
which man sought to conquer and, by the strength of his arm and
the spirit that was in him, to win through; the wind-distended,
sea-stiffened sails, blown into ribbons time and time again on the
gaunt high yards; the perilous, exhilarating, mad work upon the
rigging of the pitching terrified ship, high aloft in the shrieking gales
and the rain-filled sky; the infinitely more dangerous work on the
sea-swept exposure of the decks, from which now and again, despite
life-lines and sharp lookouts, the hands went overboard; the straining
at the open wheel, with the giant seas raging astern at which the
helmsmen did not dare to look, while they strove ceaselessly to keep
the running ship somewhere before them; the ice and the snow on
deck, and the ghastly physical misery. And then, beyond Cape Horn,
the bad weather of the winter in the South Atlantic, with more gales
and unending slavery; and afterwards, sunshine and happier skies, and
milder days and loveliness returned to a sea which did not seem
before to know of joy's existence."

13 HORRIFIED SAILORS WATCH A SHIPMATE ABOVE AS
SOME GEAR PARTS HIGH ALOFT

"The *Grace Harwar* was a dog with a bad name. Her name was near
the top of the list in my little book of ships not to sail in. She killed
someone every voyage. This was no superstition, but a matter of
cold fact. She was a killer and had been for years, washing sailors
overboard, knocking their heads off with parted wires, dropping them
out of the rigging. She was always trouble."
The Set of the Sails

14 TAKING A BIT OF SEA ABOARD ON THE WAY TO CAPE
HORN (OPPOSITE)

"Sea after sea raced ceaselessly out of the night down upon her,
roaring before the anger of the gale, and swept upon her counter and
fumed around her, and leapt up at her weather side and, now and
again, tossed hundreds of tons of themselves into the wet misery of
the main deck. Some of the seas were so big, and the ship seemed to
be driven on so furiously, that it seemed that nothing could save her
from being pooped by them, and swept helplessly fore and aft, as she
had been upon that previous occasion of the pitch of the Horn. Yet
she always rose, and she always ran on. No sea was too big for her,
and no cross-maelstrom they could devise so treacherous that she
could not run sweetly through it."

15 STANDING BY THE PINRAIL, THE SEA RUSHING
ACROSS THE DECK

"The constant battle to get our ship around the Horn had to go on,
with its never-ending work, its making fast of sails and bending new
ones, its ceaseless round of watch and watch and wet constant misery.
As the days dragged themselves by we found ourselves living for
nothing but to be past Cape Horn. Only let us come to there! we
prayed; afterwards it does not matter. Afterwards we may forget, and
think of other things. Afterwards sunshine will come and gales
will pass, and we shall feel that we are bound to England. We forgot,
down there, that there was a place called England. We were bound
only to Cape Horn."

16 HIGH ALOFT, TAKING IN SAIL AS THE STORM
INCREASES (OPPOSITE)

"Now we had also the worry of Walker's death. Working aloft is not
dangerous, in the ordinary course of events, if nothing goes wrong,
and you do not think about it. It seems dangerous enough, to those
who conjure up, from comfortable easy chairs ashore, visions of shiv-
ering sailors fighting desperately with some mad sail upon the reeling
yards of a sailing ship, driving and plunging in a gale. But if you have
seen someone get killed up on those yards it is different. You do get
nerves, after that."

17 THE CAPTAIN AND THE CHIEF MATE

18 THE STORM (OPPOSITE)

"We came to the fiftieth day, June 6th, by which I had reckoned that
we would be past the Horn, come what might. We had still 900 miles
to go. It was maddening; but what could we do about it? Nothing;
only go on. We discovered in ourselves a kind of sullen endurance, a
morbid fatalism, a capacity for standing up to the frigid horror of the
passing weeks we had not thought it possible to possess; a kind of
grim interest, so to speak, in seeing how far fate could try us.
We weren't dead, anyway. Beckman said once that if he were to be
killed he hoped he would go as Walker went. The passing days
deepened our depression, until we came to believe that we should not
come to Cape Horn, ever. Well, we would see… Cold reached the
stage where it was no longer discomfort, but acute pain. It was not
merely uncomfortable to go for one's trick to the wheel in the middle
of a sodden raining night; it was sickening torture. We sought solace
in the reflection that there could surely be no torments of hell
reserved for those who sailed in square-rigged ships, round the Horn
in winter. If there was a hell, it was warm. We would have welcomed
it… and then upon the fifty-first day – *mirabile dictu*! – there came a
west wind. It began by moaning softly through the rigging; the glass
went down steadily. We hesitated to record the fact that the west wind
had come, for fear it went again. […] But now it had come. There
was ice along the foot-ropes and in the rigging, where the spray
drove, the wind now screamed with a mad note; it whipped up the
sullen sea into a foaming madness… It became evident early that we
were in for the blow of the voyage – a regular Cape Horn hurricane."

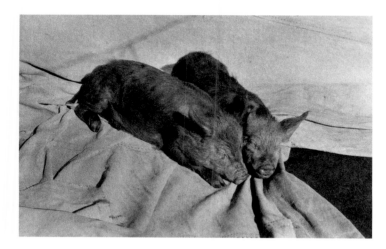

20 TWO PIGLETS SHIPPED AT WALLARRO IGNORANT OF
THE FATE AWAITING THEM: THEY DID NOT COMPLETE THE
VOYAGE, ONE WAS DROWNED, THE OTHER CONSUMED

19 MAKING TOWARDS THE HORN: ON THE MAIN MAST
FURLING THE LOWER TOPGALLANT SAIL (PRECEDING
PAGES)

21 THE SECOND MATE, THE MASTER, THE FIRST MATE
AND THE SHIP'S DOG (OPPOSITE)

"So long as we had wind we did not mind; sooner or later the Trades
would come, and our worries would be at an end. The pleasant part of
the voyage would be with us, and we could forget – could never
forget! – what had happened, but it would slip back a little in our
minds when the wind ceased to howl and the rain to weep. And then,
when we were least expecting it, when at last we thought that Fate
was through with us, it struck us a foul blow again. In a way, it was the
foulest and unfairest blow of the voyage. The second mate, a young
and splendid man, well trained in his calling and admirable in every
respect, was broken down utterly by the trials of the voyage and the
culmination of other worries from other voyages before, and suffered
so severe a nervous breakdown as to imperil his reason. It happened
with unnerving suddenness, when we were least expecting further
worries. We knew that he had been very worried since Walker died,
but so had we all; we did not think anything particularly of that.
[The second mate] has no friends at sea, because he has no equals,
and tradition rules that a man may draw his friends only from his
equals in the ship of sails. Everyone in the ship is either above or
below him. The watch is below him, in his charge. The cook, sailmaker, steward, and carpenter are petty officers, also of lesser rank.
The mate and the captain are above him, as completely as if they
belonged to another world . . . No the second mate may have no
friends. Night after night, week after week, month after month, he
must tramp the poop in his loneliness and find his company and his
pleasure in his thoughts."

22   MATES DRESSED UP FOR THE NEPTUNE CEREMONY

"On the day that we crossed the Line there was a Neptune ceremony, not that anyone felt like it, but to lift us out of our thoughts for a while and give us something else to think about, something else to do, as well as definitely to impress upon us the fact that the last stage of the voyage had been reached and there was now not much more to come... We went through the complete old wind-ship service, of Neptune hailing the ship and coming aboard over the knightheads, proceeding in state with his court and Mrs. Neptune along the deck, asking for all who had not previously entered his domain to be presented to him, and all the rest of it. There were two unfortunates who held no pass from King Neptune. These were the two Australians, who had not previously been out of their own country. They were arrested, smeared with a foul mixture of tar and grease and fish oil, shaved, ducked, and otherwise dealt with, and at the conclusion for it all forced to kiss Mrs. Neptune on the red-leaded lips. It served its purpose. They took it all in great part for the sake of the certificates of clearance to be received afterwards and because also they were fully aware of the inner meaning of the celebration."

23   LAND ON THE HORIZON — AILSA CRAIG ON STARBOARD AS THE "GRACE HARWAR" IS TOWED FROM QUEENSTOWN (FOLLOWING PAGES)

"The next day was September 1st, and we were 137 days at sea. We had been at sea half April, all May, all June, all July, all August, and now it was September, and we were still upon the road. We saw a little Irish mackerel fisherman, carrying sails; we saw a French trawler on its way to the Newfoundland banks; we saw cargo steamers thickly. The wind played us tricks again; at noon we were about 200 miles from Falmouth. Just one chance more! Just one more day of decent wind, and we would be in with the sails furled and the anchor down... The wind hauled into the south-east and freshened, and we could not head anywhere near Falmouth. Captain Svensson, in desperation, let her go off and headed up for Queenstown."

"He yarns about picturesque and other humans who have floated
through the focs'ls of ships under his command... He had a
murderer in the focs'l of the *Lawhill* on one occasion. On another
occasion, before the war, the Old Man had two firemen shanghaied
out of Newcastle, New South Wales, where there used to be almost
as much shanghaiing as in the more notorious 'Frisco'. The
difference was that in Newcastle only sailors were shanghaied, and
they were always drifters with a quaint philosophical turn of mind.
They were usually not wholly averse to being dragged aboard a ship
drunk instead of signing on in the usual way in a shipping office.
They would be drunk there, anyway: it made no difference.
One old mariner, shipped in this way, boasted that he had been at
sea forty years and had never been more than five days ashore
at a time or signed sober in a ship. He always, he said – and it was
probably true – woke up at sea after five days, and had to ask
what ship he was in and where she was going. He was never in the
least concerned whether she was a barque, a full-rigged ship, or
a five-masted schooner, bound round the Horn to Tal Tal or round
the Cape to Yokohama.
[...] It is only the during the past five years that adventurous youths,
principally belonging to nations which have no sailing ships of their
own, have so besieged the owners of the few surviving square-riggers
that the competition to secure berths lead them to pay the owner for
the privilege of working for him, instead of receiving coin of the
realm themselves for that arduous occupation."
Voyage of the Parma, 1932 voyage

8 CAPTAIN RUBEN DE CLOUX EXAMINING THE READING
ON HIS SEXTANT

"The veteran Captain de Cloux – he is forty-eight – surely presents
a good portrait of a Cape Horn shipmaster, with his old cloth cap
jammed on his massive head, his clear skin and his blue eyes,
his square, determined jaw. He is absorbed in ships and the sea; he
remembers things about ships that he has seen in ports ashore
when he remembers nothing about the ports, except perhaps the
excessive cost of discharging there, or an extortionate bill for the coal
supply of the cook's galley. At sea this ship-absorption is especially
powerful. He talks ships, thinks ships, dreams ships – this one first,
then the others of the grain fleet, and then ships in general. [...]
Upon being awakened at any time his first thought is of the ship.
He spends all day and half the night on the poop watching,
watching, watching – ship, ship, ship! In bad weather he stands
by the forepart of the chart-house (the weather-cloth has been blown
away), chocked off there by the water-tank which stands between
the house and the bole of the jigger mast. Hail lashes him, spray
and rain wet him through and through, the wind roars round him,
and the crashing of the seas breaking on board thunders in his ears:
he stands on, swaying from foot to foot with her roll, watching her,
considering how she sails, how she might be better sailed; surveying
the set of her canvas, the cant of her yards; ruminating upon the
strength of her, absorbing her every motion, storing away this
priceless sea lore in his grey head to be used upon future occasions.
A sailor, he says, can always learn about ships; to know any ship it
is necessary to sail four years in her and to study her closely during
that time. To imagine that one knows everything, that the sea has no
more to teach and the mind no more to learn, is certain prelude to
disaster. He is always learning."
Voyage of the Parma, 1932 voyage

16 AT THE CAPSTAN, THE SEA BREAKING ON BOARD

15 THE SEA SMASHES DRIVING SPRAYS ACROSS THE
WAIST (OPPOSITE)

"All at once a tremendous sea lifted our stern high in the air and we
were sent driving ahead at a great speed. She kept right on going and
drove her bow clean under, taking the sea as it stood fair over the
focs'l head. It came over our heads and right down in front of us, just
as if we were at the bottom of Niagara Falls inside the water looking
out. I saw the next sea break high over the poop, and the main-deck
was full of water pouring in on her from all directions at once,
which held her down. She went down and down – sinking until we
felt it in our stomachs badly, although she had been going through
some tricks before. She began to settle to port and went over until the
end of the main-yard seemed as if it was in the water. We scrambled
out as best we could and tried to get to the rigging, many of us
believing that she was going right over. I did not see how she could
come up again. She was swung now broadside to the seas. I did not
think that big ships could do a thing like this and get away with it;
I thought I was being given an unpleasant demonstration of what
happened to missing ships..."
Voyage of the Parma, 1932 voyage

"It is curious how the perspective changes here, abaft the mast. The very aspect of the sails, of the masts and yards, is different; the motion of the ship is not the same as in the for'ard house. Here one feels her lurches more, and her pitches; every move she makes is immediately felt in the poop. For'ard in the big house she has to lunge wildly or dip steeply before it is felt much, if at all. Here one sees the ship as a handful of officers doing a master's bidding, with two houses full of youths on deck who do the work, and a cook to cook, a steward to look after the provisions and so forth, a sailmaker to sew sails, and a carpenter for the blacksmithing and the carpentry. To one of the youths in either for'ard house the aspect was entirely different.

What is the ship, we ask, but a great wheat stack of some 5,000 tons with a steel shell around it, thirty-one human beings living on top, and masts and sails to give the lot propulsion? What indeed? But the conglomeration takes a great deal of getting to England."

Voyage of the Parma, 1932 voyage

18 APPRENTICES ON THE BOWSPRIT

"The long uncertainty of this voyage makes getting into Falmouth
at the end tremendously worth while; we have no way of finding out
anything until we come up. It is the custom then for the skippers
to write round to one another, giving details of their voyages, their
best day's run, number of days, luck off the Horn and in the Trades,
and so on, and in that way the real news of the race goes round.
In few newspapers is it ever reported accurately, partly because
newspaper reporters, in their hurry for news, are frequently misled
by over-zealous enthusiasts in the different vessels who are plagued by
an irresistible desire to magnify the performance of their own ship
and to belittle that of all others."
Voyage of the Parma, 1932 voyage

19 THE LEE SIDE (FOLLOWING PAGES)

"With a strong westerly we could overhaul that steamer... With
night-fall we are quite becalmed, with bright moonlight, stars, clear
sky, and moderate swell. What do we want with calms here? If we
have gained any advantage over the others by those storms South of
fifty – and we are by no means sure that we have – now they will
dribble down on us and our light lead is lost. Our tactics go for
nothing, and all our troubles are in vain. Another ship two days
behind us can sail up on us now, if we lie two days here. Then after
sailing for more than 6,000 miles we shall set off level again and by
our faster sailing (if of course, it existed – we only like to think it does)
we shall only first have reached the calm. Let calms stay in the Horse-
latitudes and on the Line where they belong, we growl, resentful
of the efficiency of the steamer's thudding propeller. We talk of
turning back for Good Hope from here, 300 miles from the Horn.
We could go northwards along the Chilean coast until we struck the
S.E. Trades of the Pacific, and then head due west until we came to
Torres Straits, and so on through there round the north of Australia
and into the S.E. Trades of the Indian Ocean, and across to the
Mozambique Channel and round Good Hope with the favouring
Agulhas current... At midnight the same.
Wednesday, April 20. Thirty-four days... Calm and light easterly airs
all day. This *is* maddening."
Voyage of the Parma, 1932 voyage

"We came past the Horn itself at eventide with the moon almost
full, silvering the black waters: gently we sailed by still with our
royals. Black under the moon, rising bluntly like the head of a sperm
whale to its snow-surmounted summit, the dreaded bulk of the
massive Cape stood solemn in a quiet sea. It is not often quiet here!
Many ships and many sailors lie buried here. Nobody knows when
the most of them died. They set out bravely from some port, bound
round the Horn, and they never came in from the sea again, nor
were heard of. [...] The list of missing ships is incredibly long; in
sail, Cape Horn is responsible for half of them. Three deep they lie
around us as we sail beneath the moon; the iron and the steel of their
battered hulls is scattered by the sea rim of these gaunt hills; the
bones of their sailors lie somewhere here beneath the quiet surface
of the deceptive sea."
Voyage of the Parma, 1932 voyage

27 THE SAILS BLOWN OUT, DRIVING ALONG (PRECEDING PAGES)

28 GOING ALOFT, CLIMBING THE STARBOARD FORE SHROUDS

"In 1930 only eight big sailing ships were chartered for Australian grain; in 1931 there were twelve; in 1932 and 1933, however, conditions were better, and twenty ships were chartered in both of those years. As recently as 1921 there were 140. The other 120 ships are gone and will never be replaced; the Finnish remnant must soon follow them. They are old and their days are numbered, and when they are gone there will be no more. The freight trains will thunder on and the airplanes roar, but the wind will not sigh again gently in the rigging of an old sailing ship, wandering quietly through the Trades; the sun will not shine again upon billowed sails swelling peacefully above rusted hulls; beauty will be gone from the ocean, and an art-form lost to the world.
How soon? In five years, perhaps; certainly in no more than ten."
Last of the Wind Ships, 1933 voyage

FOLLOWING PAGES

29 A STRONG PULL AND A LONG PULL

"We have come to June 1, and are going splendidly. We have the N.E. Trade, fine and fresh, and make from 160 to 200 miles a day. We hope it keeps up, and are thankful for the good days as they come. We still have some prospect of a passage of less than 100 days. The Old Man hopes that we shall cross the thirtieth parallel of North latitude 81 days out, and be from 14 to 16 days from up there. All the voyage we have been hoping. That is all we do – make the best of each day's breeze as it comes, and go on hoping. It is much cooler now, and bare backs are no longer comfortable; yet we have not caught up with the sun. We are pleased to be spared the sweltering heat usually associated with the Tropics. We can do without it."
Voyage of the Parma, 1932 voyage

30 LOOKING ALOFT FROM THE BOWSPRIT

"He recalls also strange happenings of the sea in his experience – how once in another small barque a boy was seen to go aloft, and was never seen to come down again nor fall, nor was he ever found anywhere, from that hour; how in the same vessel another sailor fell from the bowsprit taking in a jib, was sailed over by the length of the ship, came up astern with a split head, and was promptly hauled aboard by the astonished skipper! She nearly pooped as the figure came up beneath her; he was almost drowned, of course, but he lived, and was back at work again within a few days… He recalls also the strange case of a sailor in another barque who, seated calmly on the rail one day in good weather, asked the mate for the loan of a steel snatch-block so that he could tie it on his legs and jump overboard. The mate, thinking it was a joke, said he could have the block, and all hands looked on with amusement while he tied it to his legs. Then the sailor slipped over the side and went down like a stone. No one knew any reason why he should wish to commit suicide; and nobody was amused then."
Voyage of the Parma, 1932 voyage

36 THE LEE BOW

"In the calm we put out a boat and pulled around old *Parma*. How
big she is! Used for so long to her decks and her rigging, she seems
like a strange ship from outside. She is big, and black, and rusty; as
she lifts in the swells she shows the red boot-topping gone from
her under-side, and the white anti-fouling of the nitrate-carrier
showing through. [. . .] The sea, so small from the big vessel, is huge
to us now; we fall in the troughs and see nothing of our *Parma* but
her rigging, only a ship's length away. We are stirred by the beauty
of the ship, just lying there in the calm, and we lie there on the oars
and look at her while she drifts slowly on. She is very big and her
masts are not high. She is not a clipper. She is a big hard-working,
economic windjammer, sail's last effort against steams. But she
has loveliness and grace; she follows nobly in the traditions of the best
of sail, and blends perfectly into the peace of her surroundings."
Voyage of the Parma, 1932 voyage

35 LOOKING ALOFT ON THE MIZZEN, THE INTERLACING
STAYS SUPPORTING THE MAST (OPPOSITE)

" 'I like beautiful things – lovely women and tall sailing ships,
sunsets and wisps of smoke rising from the farmer's home upon some
quiet countryside,' writes a man in a magazine who probably never
saw a vessel under canvas. The pictures of them appeal to him. I look
up at the masts and yards from the boat; the man is right. There is
such a grace and quiet loveliness about this ship as we like to think
there is about beautiful women. Everything about her matched
perfectly: her curves, her angles, her posture upon the water, the set
of masts and yards, until the whole is a creation of symmetrical
loveliness that the mind is better for the eye's beholding. She looks
restful (not always!), faithful, true – demanding only understanding."
Voyage of the Parma, 1932 voyage

"The cook's day begins at four a.m. and ends at nine in the evening.
On alternate mornings the steward arose at four and the cook at six:
this was a good arrangement. The steward looked after the food and
baked the bread [...] The most hopeless of his occupations (and he
had many) was trying to get young Moses to work. This was a pursuit
that might as well have been abandoned. Moses, the loud-voiced,
the cheeky little boy, the attractive, brown-haired, soft-eyed, devilish,
prank-playing, work-avoiding youngster: Moses, the Dresden devil
(as the mate called him), might as well be left to his own devices.
Moses began all things and finished none; the more useless they were,
the more quickly he began them. His duties were those of cabin-boy –
to wash dishes and scrub cabins, and carry food. Moses ate the food,
catlicked the cabins hastily once weekly, and invariable had the dishes
from the last meal washed just in time for the next. Moses ate more
than anyone else in the ship, and lamented continually that the only
thing wrong on earth (beside the oppression of the Germans) was the
sad fact that the human stomach had been made too small. If we all
had bigger stomachs, said Moses, there would be much more peace.
Which may be true. Indeed, a general enlargement of the world's
stomachs (together with the wherewithal to line them) might go as
far as any other means towards the establishment of lasting peace.
Not that Moses was overmuch concerned with peace. To his arsenal
of weapons from the precious voyage he had added an automatic
pistol that fortunately would not work; in any case, he had used up
all his ammunition firing at albatrosses. Moses, at the age of fourteen,
or whatever he was (we did not know exactly), had been an apprentice
in a Hamburg delicatessen (where he was fired in the process of
unduly enlarging his small stomach with the proprietor's foods),
a rumrunner in a Hungarian trawler in the Gulf of Bothnia, and an
inmate of the Stockholm gaol. There he caused so much disturbance
that they threw him out, whereupon he became apprenticed to the
Parma with the proceeds of his nefarious exploits."
Last of the Wind Ships, 1933 voyage

47 ELISABETH JACOBSEN (CENTRE), CAPTAIN DE CLOUX
AND HIS DAUGHTER RUBY

"In 1933, fourteen four-masted barques were competing, together
with a full-rigged ship, a four-masted barquentine, and four barques
[...] The *Parma*, which had made the best passages both outwards
and homewards the previous year, compared poorly with the others
with an outward run of 96 days; even the *Olivebank* and the little
Favell could better that. But the *Parma* had been jammed in the
North Sea by the Channel mouth with west winds, when the others
had gone north of Scotland to find a kinder breeze: besides the Old
Man had taken his young daughter with him to sea, and women at sea
have proverbially meant bad luck.

At least so the boy-crew said. Women at sea are bad luck, they
averred: women, and parsons, and dead bodies, in that order.
They ascribed the whole 'blame' for the crack's long passage to
the Old Man's seventeen-year-old daughter, and wandered around
the decks gloomily expecting the ship to be at least 200 days getting
to England. At the loading port in Spencer Gulf another young girl
joined the ship's company; and at that the boys gave themselves up
entirely to melancholy forebodings. Nor did they abandon their
expectations of disaster until the anchor was down in Falmouth Bay –
expectations which were entirely baseless since the *Parma* made a
record passage and did not lose a sail!"

Last of the Wind Ships, 1933 voyage

49 ELISABETH JACOBSEN EXAMINING A MODEL OF THE
"PARMA"

48 THE MODELMAKER WORKING ON A CAPSTAN HEAD
(OPPOSITE)

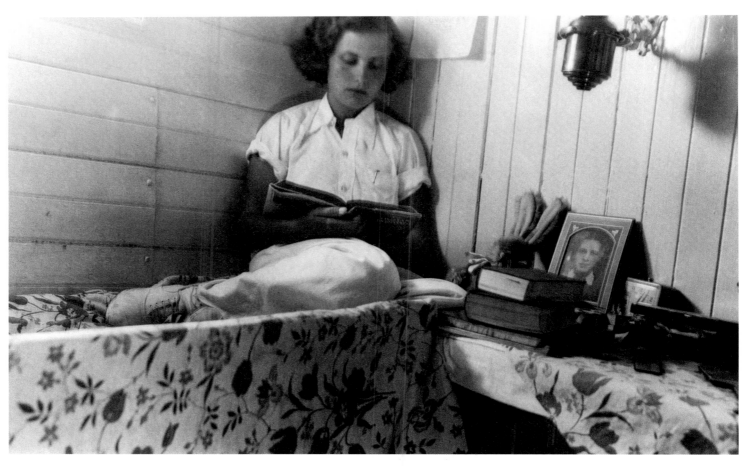

50 ELISABETH JACOBSEN IN HER BUNK

52 "MOZART" AND "PENANG", TWO OF THE GRAIN-RACERS
(FOLLOWING PAGES)

"What of the race? How did that end? Now all the ships have some
in – those that are still afloat – and I write in retrospect. The
Hougomont was dismasted on the outward voyage; the *Melbourne* will
never come in from the sea again, for a steamer cut her down and her
bones and half her people lie buried deep where the North Atlantic
swirls not far from Queenstown heads. With her voyage done and
her landfall made, she was sent to her doom so quickly that she
sank without losing way, and her officers and her crew died looking
forward to their mail upon the morrow.

The *Pommern* and the *Mozart* were on the reinsurance list before
they came in, rusty and barnacled. They were so much overdue that
the insurers of their cargoes – they are not themselves insured – grew
alarmed, and covered their risks with new premiums. The *Mozart*
went to 15 per cent; then she came in, with a passage of 151 days.
She had not been reported or heard from during the whole of the
five months."

Voyage of the Parma, 1932 voyage

51 THE STEAMER "SANTAROSA" LEAVES US, SWINGING
AWAY ON HER COURSE FOR THE UNITED STATES

"We saw some fishing schooners going to the Grand Banks; the sea
greyed again and the blue sky dulled, and we saw oil-tanks and such
prosaic vessels outward bound. They waddled by and took no notice.
It was not until we were almost within sight of England that we saw
the barque *Penang*, the first grain-racer we had met in the whole
passage. [...] The next day we were in England. Eighty-three days!
There had not been a passage like it in this century."
Last of the Wind Ships, 1933 voyage

53 WEIGHING THE ANCHOR (PRECEDING PAGES)

54 JOURNEY'S END: DRYING SAIL WAITING TO BE DOCKED

"And so we were docked at last; and all the sharks, butchers, tailors, compass-adjustors, and candlestick makers of Cardiff came aboard until it was difficult to move about the decks, and customs men with watery eyes drink what is left of the Old Man's whisky and harass and torment the personnel and the ship. Smoke belches at us from the steamers moored all round, and men in brassbound uniforms shriek and shout orders through megaphones, and trains rattle over bridges, and coal dust fills the air, and idlers troop down in their hundreds to gaze up at the gauntness of the sail-stripped yards in wide-eyed wonder, and gape and say they would sooner be dead than sail in such a ship as ours.

[…] We look aloft for the last time at the tall masts with their massive yards, scientific creation for the use of God's wind and the delivery of sweet ships from the ocean. Now the land breeze stirs quietly in the rigging, where already the grime of port is settling, and it is time to go. From the quayside we look back at her, loath to depart: she looks powerful and huge in the docks; yet she looks depressed, too, with the buildings all round, the bumbledom officials harrying her, and a lamppost with a lifebuoy slung from it jammed under her counter. Brave old ship! Aloft the boys, unbending the maint'gallants'ls, wave to us in the sunshine… and somehow, in a curious kind of a way, one feels that one is not yet finished with Cape Horners."

Voyage of the Parma, 1932 voyage

55 CHIPPING RUST AT CARDIFF QUAYSIDE (FOLLOWING PAGES)